Accounting Changes
and Error Corrections

Steven M. Bragg

AccountingTools®

ISBN 978-1-64221-291-4

For more information about AccountingTools® products, visit our Web site at www.accountingtools.com.

Table of Contents

About the Author

Steven Bragg, CPA, has been the chief financial officer or controller of four companies, as well as a consulting manager at Ernst & Young. He received a master's degree in finance from Bentley College, an MBA from Babson College, and a Bachelor's degree in Economics from the University of Maine. He has been a two-time president of the Colorado Mountain Club, and is an avid alpine skier, mountain biker, and certified master diver. Mr. Bragg resides in Centennial, Colorado. He has written more than 300 books and courses, including *New Controller Guidebook*, *GAAP Guidebook*, and *Payroll Management*.

Steven maintains the accountingtools.com web site, which contains continuing professional education courses, the Accounting Best Practices podcast, and thousands of articles on accounting subjects.

Buy Additional AccountingTools Courses

AccountingTools offers more than 1,500 hours of CPE courses, with concentrations in accounting, auditing, finance, taxation, and ethics. Related courses that you might like include:

- Accountant's Guidebook
- Bookkeeping Guidebook
- New Controller Guidebook

Go to accountingtools.com/cpe to view these additional courses.

AccountingTools®

Accounting Changes and Error Corrections

Introduction

From time to time, a company will find that it must alter its accounting to reflect a change in accounting principle or estimate, or it may locate an accounting error that must be corrected. These changes can have a substantial impact on the reported results of a business from period to period, which can make financial statements much less comparable over time. Examples of these changes are:

- An organization switches from reporting its sale transactions as gross sales to net sales, reflecting the finding that the business is really operating as an agent for another party. The effect is a drastic decline in the amount of reported sales.
- An entity switches its inventory costing method from the first in, first out method to the weighted average method, which results in a one-time increase in the value of ending inventory, which in turn boosts net income.
- A firm evaluates its accounts receivable and concludes that a sudden decline in general economic conditions will drastically increase the amount of bad debts it will experience. This calls for a doubling of the balance in the allowance for doubtful accounts, which reduces profits.

In this manual, we address the rules pertaining to accounting changes and error corrections and how to disclose them, as well as several related situations. The guidance in this manual applies to the financial statements issued by all entities. It also applies to historical summaries of information that are based on financial statements, such as the five-year and ten-year histories of financial results frequently found in annual reports.

Changes in Accounting Principle

Accounting principles are the rules and guidelines that an entity must follow when reporting financial information. There is an assumption in generally accepted accounting principles (GAAP) that, once an accounting principle has been adopted by a business, the principle shall be consistently applied in recording transactions and events from that point forward. Consistent application is a cornerstone of accounting, since it allows the readers of financial statements to compare the results of multiple accounting periods. Given how important it is to maintain consistency in the application of accounting principles, a business should only change a principle in one of the two following situations:

- The change is required by an update to GAAP. In recent years, a number of GAAP updates have required changes in accounting principle, such as new standards on revenue recognition, fair value measurement, and business combinations. There are any number of industry-specific standards that are also changed; common targets for these changes are the real estate, financial services, and health care industries.

- The use of an alternative principle is preferable. There are a small number of situations in which there are two or more alternative applications of GAAP that can be used, depending on a number of indicators. If the circumstances of a business change, the indicators could point toward the use of an alternative principle. For example, a business has previously recognized its sales at gross, but its increasing control by a manufacturer indicates that sales should instead be recognized at net, as would be used by an agent.

> **Tip:** Thoroughly document the reason for any change in accounting principle, since it will likely be reviewed and possibly contested by the company's auditors. There should be a clearly defensible reason for the change.

Whenever there is a change in accounting principle, retrospective application of the new principle to prior accounting periods is required, unless it is impracticable to do so. Retrospective application means that a principle must be used as the basis for creating financial statements as though the principle had always been used for all periods presented. If it is impracticable to retroactively apply changes to prior interim periods of the current fiscal year, then the change in accounting principle can only be made as of the start of a subsequent fiscal year.

> **Tip:** Where possible, companies are encouraged to adopt changes in accounting principle as of the first interim period of a fiscal year, so that the change covers the entire fiscal year. This makes interim periods more comparable throughout a fiscal year.

The activities required for retrospective application are:

1. Alter the carrying amounts of assets and liabilities for the cumulative effect of the change in principle as of the beginning of the first accounting period presented.
2. Adjust the beginning balance of retained earnings to offset the change noted in the first step.
3. Adjust the financial statements for each prior period presented to reflect the impact of the new accounting principle.

If it is impracticable to make these changes, then do so as of the earliest reported periods for which it is practicable to do so. It is considered impracticable to make a retrospective change when any of the following conditions apply:

- *Assumptions.* Making a retrospective application calls for assumptions about what management intended to do in prior periods, and those assumptions cannot be independently substantiated.

- *Efforts made.* The company has made every reasonable effort to enact a retrospective change.
- *Estimates.* Estimates are required, which are impossible to provide due to the lack of information available when the prior-period financial statements were issued and evidence of the circumstances that existed at that time.

EXAMPLE

The Billabong Machining Company maintains a large number of old-style engine parts that it maintains for the automotive after-market. The company has been using the first in, first out (FIFO) method, but management has decided to switch to the last in, first out (LIFO) method. In order to incorporate this change in accounting principle into the financial statements for prior years, the accounting staff would have to derive assumptions regarding the periods in which different LIFO cost layers occurred, which cannot be independently substantiated. Consequently, the change is made on a go-forward basis.

The preceding retrospective application is required, except in situations where there are explicit transition requirements related to the introduction of a new accounting standard.

When making prior period adjustments due to a change in accounting principle, do so only for the direct effects of the change, net of tax. A direct effect is a recognized change in an asset or liability that is *required* in order to switch to the use of a different accounting principle. An indirect effect is one that *results from* a change in accounting principle that is applied retrospectively.

EXAMPLE

Armadillo Industries changes from the last in, first out method of inventory accounting to the first in, first out method. Doing so calls for an increase in the ending inventory in the preceding period, which in turn increases net profits for that period. Altering the inventory balance is a direct effect of the change in principle.

An indirect effect of the change in principle would be a change in the corporate accrual for profit sharing in the prior period, since the change will impact profits. Since it is an indirect effect, Armadillo does not record the change.

Note: When an organization initially adopts an accounting principle, this is not considered a change in accounting principle – it is simply the first time that an event has arisen that requires the use of the principle.

Disadvantages of Retrospective Application

The requirement to retrospectively apply changes in accounting principle can present several difficult issues for the accounting department and the readers of an organization's financial statements. These issues include:

- *Confusion.* There can be confusion among the recipients of an entity's financial statements when the newest version of a financial statement varies from one that was previously released. This issue can be mitigated by sending an accompanying note to recipients, asking them to destroy the previous version of the financials.
- *Contractual effects.* A business may have agreed to certain loan covenants that require it to meet liquidity or other targets. If a retrospective change is made, a business might find that it has been out of compliance with a loan agreement for a considerable period of time, which could lead to some interesting discussions with the lender.
- *Work load.* The task of making retrospective changes can be complex, since prior periods must be re-opened in the accounting software and altered.

Changes in Accounting Estimate

A change in accounting estimate occurs when there is an adjustment to the carrying amount of an asset or liability, or the subsequent accounting for it. Examples of changes in accounting estimate are changes in:

- The allowance for doubtful accounts
- The reserve for obsolete inventory
- The useful life of depreciable assets
- The salvage values of depreciable assets
- The amount of expected warranty obligations
- Actuarial assumptions related to pensions
- The quantities of mineral reserves yet to be depleted

Changes in accounting estimate occur relatively frequently, and so would require a major amount of effort to make an ongoing series of retroactive changes to prior financial statements. Instead, GAAP only requires that changes in accounting estimate be accounted for in the period of change and thereafter (which is *prospective* application). Thus, no retrospective change is required or allowed. Also, do not issue pro forma financial statements for prior periods that show what the effects of a change in accounting estimate would have been.

EXAMPLE

The controller of Grunge Motor Sports notes that a downward trend in general economic conditions has increased the probability that Grunge's customers will not pay. This leads her to alter the original estimation that 1.2% of all accounts receivable will eventually be charged off as bad debts. Her new estimate is 1.4% of all receivables, which results in the following entry.

	Debit	Credit
Bad debt expense (expense)	28,000	
Allowance for doubtful accounts (contra asset)		28,000

This is a change in accounting estimate, so it is accounted for in the period of change.

There may be cases in which a change in accounting estimate is indistinguishable from a change in accounting principle. When this situation arises, it should be accounted for as a change in accounting estimate. For example, a business may have previously deferred certain costs and recognized them in later periods, but now elects to charge them to expense, on the grounds that their future benefit is no longer clear. In this case, a new method of accounting is being used to accelerate expense recognition, but the reason for it is that the underlying estimation method can no longer be trusted.

EXAMPLE

The controller of Inscrutable Corporation is evaluating the company's fixed assets, and concludes that the pattern of consumption of these assets argues in favor of switching to an accelerated depreciation method from the current straight-line method. Though a different calculation method will now be used for depreciation, the reason for it is based on a change in accounting estimate that is derived from new information. This change should be accounted for on a prospective basis, with no retrospective application.

Disadvantages of Prospective Application

When there are changes in accounting estimates, the financial statements to which these changes have been prospectively applied (i.e., on a go-forward basis) are no longer comparable to those financial statements that were already issued prior to the prospective application. This is usually not considered to be a major issue, since changes in accounting estimate tend to have immaterial effects on the financial statements.

Changes in Reporting Entity

There are situations where a change in the entities included in consolidated financial statements effectively means that there is a change in the reporting entity. For example:

- Consolidated results are presented instead of the financial statements of an individual entity.
- There is a change in the specific subsidiaries that comprise a group of businesses for which consolidated financial statements are being presented.

In these situations, apply the change in reporting entity retrospectively to all of the periods being reported. The result should be the consistent presentation of financial information for the same reporting entity for all periods, including interim periods. This presentation allows for historical trend analysis across all of the reporting periods.

There are a number of situations that are not considered a change in reporting entity. For example:

- A change in the legal structure of an existing entity is not considered a change in reporting entity. For example, a change from a C corporation to an S corporation does not require the application of the accounting for changes in reporting entity.
- A business combination accounted for using the acquisition method is not a change in reporting entity; there is no retroactive consolidation with the financial statements of the acquiree for any periods presented that are prior to the acquisition date.

Correction of an Error in Previously Issued Financial Statements

From time to time, financial statements will be inadvertently issued that contain one or more errors. The following are considered to be errors:

- A mathematical miscalculation
- A mistake in the application of GAAP
- The misuse of facts existing when the financial statements were prepared

A change from an unacceptable accounting principle to a generally accepted accounting principle is considered to be the correction of an error. For example, switching from the cash basis of accounting to the accrual basis of accounting (which is recognized under GAAP) is considered to be the correction of an error.

When an error is discovered, the prior period financial statements to which the error applies must be restated. A restatement involves the revision of previously-issued financial statements. Restatement requires the following steps:

1. Alter the carrying amounts of assets and liabilities for the cumulative effect of the error as of the beginning of the first accounting period presented.
2. Adjust the beginning balance of retained earnings to offset the change noted in the first step.
3. Adjust the financial statements for each prior period presented to reflect the impact of the error.

EXAMPLE

The controller of Kelvin Corporation is reviewing depreciation records, and finds that the depreciation for certain manufacturing equipment has been incorrectly calculated for the past five years, resulting in a depreciation expense that is cumulatively too low by $82,000. She creates the following adjustment to correct the error:

	Debit	Credit
Retained earnings (equity)	82,000	
Accumulated depreciation (contra asset)		82,000

EXAMPLE

A customer of International Automation pays the company $60,000, which is intended to pay for an automation consulting project that spans the end of 20X3 and the beginning of 20X4, with two-thirds of the work to be completed in 20X4. The accounting staff inadvertently recognizes the entire payment as revenue in 20X3. The correcting entry is:

	Debit	Credit
Retained earnings (equity)	40,000	
Deferred revenue (liability)		40,000

The correction of an error is not the same as an accounting change. An accounting change, as noted earlier, involves either a change in estimate or a change in accounting principle.

Corrections Related to Prior Interim Periods

An interim period is a financial reporting period that is shorter than a full fiscal year, such as a three-month reporting period. GAAP specifies several situations in which the financial statements of prior interim periods of the current fiscal year should be adjusted. These adjustments are for the following:

- Adjustment or settlement of litigation

- Income taxes
- Renegotiation proceedings
- Utility revenue under rate-making processes

Adjustments for these items are only necessary if all of the following criteria apply:

- The effect of the change is material to income from continuing operations, or its trend
- The adjustments are directly related to the prior interim periods
- The adjustment amount could not be reasonably estimated prior to the current interim period, but can now be estimated

If an adjustment occurs in any interim period other than the first period, use the following steps to account for it:

1. Include any portion of the adjustment that relates to current business activities in the current interim period.
2. Restate prior interim periods of the current fiscal year to include that portion of the item that relates to the business activities in those periods.
3. Restate the first interim period of the current fiscal year to include that portion of the item that relates to the business activities in prior fiscal years.

The Materiality of an Error

When an accounting error is discovered, determine whether it is material enough to report. To do so, compare its effect to the full-year estimated income or the full-year earnings trend. If it is not material, there is no need to disclose it. However, if the error is material in relation to the estimated income or earnings trend for an interim period, disclose the error in the financial statements for that interim period.

EXAMPLE

Armadillo Industries has profits of $1,000,000 in its first quarter, and expects to generate $4,000,000 of profits for the entire fiscal year. The company has historically considered materiality to be 5% of its profits. In the first quarter, the accounting department uncovers a $100,000 error. Though this amount is 10% of first-quarter profits, it is only 2.5% of full-year expected profits. Given the minimal impact on full-year profits, Armadillo does not have to segregate this information for reporting purposes in its first quarter interim reporting, though it must still disclose the information.

The Materiality Principle

The preceding directive in this section to report a material error does not describe the parameters of materiality. This is a concept that is difficult to pin down, since GAAP does not provide a clear definition of what is material or immaterial. One way to view materiality is through the materiality principle, which is based on general usage.

Under this principle, an item is considered to be material if it is probable that users of the financial statements would have altered their actions if certain information had not been in error. If users would not have altered their actions, then the error is said to be immaterial.

The SEC's View of Materiality

The Securities and Exchange Commission has a conservative view of how to deal with the materiality concept, which it has stated in its staff accounting bulletins (SABs). An SAB is a summarization of the views of the SEC staff regarding how GAAP is to be applied. The views stated in an SAB are followed by the staffs of the Office of the Chief Accountant and the Division of Corporate Finance when reviewing the filings of publicly-held companies. For this reason, SABs are closely adhered to by entities registering their securities within the United States. If a publicly-held company does not incorporate the concepts in these bulletins into their financial statements and disclosures, it may receive a comment letter from the SEC.

The following two issues related to materiality have been addressed by the SEC in an SAB. The text is a slightly compressed version of the full SEC discussion. In essence, the SEC's views on materiality might lead an accountant to engage in a relatively detailed analysis of most issues, with a higher resulting probability that issues must be recognized in the financial statements.

Situation: During the course of preparing or auditing year-end financial statements, financial management or the company's independent auditor becomes aware of misstatements in the company's financial statements. When combined, the misstatements result in a 4% overstatement of net income and a $.02 (4%) overstatement of earnings per share. Because no item in the company's consolidated financial statements is misstated by more than 5%, management and the independent auditor conclude that the deviation from GAAP is immaterial and that the accounting is permissible.

In the staff's view, may a company or the auditor of its financial statements assume the immateriality of items that fall below a percentage threshold set by management or the auditor to determine whether amounts and items are material to the financial statements? No. The SEC is aware that certain companies, over time, have developed quantitative thresholds as "rules of thumb" to assist in the preparation of their financial statements, and that auditors also have used these thresholds in their evaluation of whether items might be considered material to users of a company's financial statements. One rule of thumb in particular suggests that the misstatement or omission of an item that falls under a 5% threshold is not material in the absence of particularly egregious circumstances, such as self-dealing or misappropriation by senior management. The SEC reminds companies and the auditors of their financial statements that exclusive reliance on this or any percentage or numerical threshold has no basis in the accounting literature or the law.

The use of a percentage as a numerical threshold, such as 5%, may provide the basis for a preliminary assumption that a deviation of less than the specified percentage with respect to a particular item on the company's financial statements is unlikely to be material. The SEC has no objection to such a "rule of thumb" as an initial step in assessing materiality. But quantifying, in percentage terms, the magnitude of a misstatement is only the beginning of an analysis of materiality; it cannot appropriately be used as a substitute for a full analysis of all relevant considerations. Materiality concerns the significance of an item to users of a company's financial statements. A matter is "material" if there is a substantial likelihood that a reasonable person would consider it important.

As a result of the interaction of quantitative and qualitative considerations in materiality judgments, misstatements of relatively small amounts that come to the auditor's attention could have a material effect on the financial statements. Among the considerations that may well render material a quantitatively small misstatement of a financial statement item are the following:

- Whether the misstatement arises from an item capable of precise measurement or whether it arises from an estimate and, if so, the degree of imprecision inherent in the estimate
- Whether the misstatement masks a change in earnings or other trends
- Whether the misstatement hides a failure to meet analysts' consensus expectations for the enterprise
- Whether the misstatement changes a loss into income or vice versa
- Whether the misstatement concerns a segment or other portion of the company's business that has been identified as playing a significant role in the company's operations or profitability
- Whether the misstatement affects the company's compliance with regulatory requirements
- Whether the misstatement affects the company's compliance with loan covenants or other contractual requirements
- Whether the misstatement has the effect of increasing management's compensation; for example, by satisfying requirements for the award of bonuses or other forms of incentive compensation
- Whether the misstatement involves concealment of an unlawful transaction

For the reasons noted above, a company and the auditors of its financial statements should not assume that even small intentional misstatements in financial statements, for example those pursuant to actions to "manage" earnings, are immaterial.

The materiality of a misstatement may turn on where it appears in the financial statements. For example, a misstatement may involve a segment of the company's operations. In that instance, in assessing materiality of a misstatement to the financial statements taken as a whole, companies and their auditors should consider not only the size of the misstatement but also the significance of the segment information to the financial statements taken as a whole.

In determining whether multiple misstatements cause the financial statements to be materially misstated, companies and the auditors of their financial statements should consider each misstatement separately and the aggregate effect of all misstatements. If the misstatement of an individual amount causes the financial statements as a whole to be materially misstated, that effect cannot be eliminated by other misstatements whose effect may be to diminish the impact of the misstatement on other financial statement items. To take an obvious example, if a company's revenues are a material financial statement item and if they are materially overstated, the financial statements taken as a whole will be materially misleading even if the effect on earnings is completely offset by an equivalent overstatement of expenses.

Even though a misstatement of an individual amount may not cause the financial statements taken as a whole to be materially misstated, it may nonetheless, when aggregated with other misstatements, render the financial statements taken as a whole to be materially misleading. Companies and the auditors of their financial statements accordingly should consider the effect of the misstatement on subtotals or totals. The auditor should aggregate all misstatements that affect each subtotal or total and consider whether the misstatements in the aggregate affect the subtotal or total in a way that causes the company's financial statements taken as a whole to be materially misleading.

Companies and auditors also should consider the effect of misstatements from prior periods on the current financial statements. This may be particularly the case where immaterial misstatements recur in several years and the cumulative effect becomes material in the current year.

Situation: During the course of preparing annual financial statements, a company is evaluating the materiality of an improper expense accrual (e.g., overstated liability) in the amount of $100, which has built up over 5 years, at $20 per year. The company previously evaluated the misstatement as being immaterial to each of the prior year financial statements (i.e., years 1-4). For the purpose of evaluating materiality in the current year (i.e., year 5), the company quantifies the error as a $20 overstatement of expenses.

Has the company appropriately quantified the amount of this error for the purpose of evaluating materiality for the current year? No. In this example, the company has only quantified the effects of the identified unadjusted error that arose in the current year income statement. Prior year misstatements should be considered in quantifying misstatements in current year financial statements.

The techniques most commonly used in practice to accumulate and quantify misstatements are generally referred to as the "rollover" and "iron curtain" approaches. The rollover approach, which is the approach used in the example, quantifies a misstatement based on the amount of the error originating in the current year income statement. This approach ignores the effects of correcting the portion of the current year balance sheet misstatement that originated in prior years (i.e., it ignores the "carryover effects" of prior year misstatements). The iron curtain approach quantifies a misstatement based on the effects of correcting the misstatement existing in the balance sheet at the end of the current year, irrespective of the misstatement's year(s) of origination. Had the company in this fact pattern applied the iron curtain approach, the misstatement would have been quantified as a $100 misstatement based on the end of year balance sheet misstatement. Thus, the adjustment needed to correct the financial statements for the end of year error would be to reduce the liability by $100 with a corresponding decrease in current year expense.

As demonstrated in this example, the primary weakness of the rollover approach is that it can result in the accumulation of significant misstatements on the balance sheet that are deemed immaterial in part because the amount that originates in each year is quantitatively small.

In contrast, the primary weakness of the iron curtain approach is that it does not consider the correction of prior year misstatements in the current year (i.e., the reversal of the carryover effects) to be errors. Therefore, in this example, if the misstatement was corrected during the current year such that no error existed in the balance sheet at the end of the current year, the reversal of the $80 prior year misstatement would not be considered an error in the current year financial statements under the iron curtain approach. Implicitly, the iron curtain approach assumes that because the prior year financial statements were not materially misstated, correcting any immaterial errors that existed in those statements in the current year is the "correct" accounting, and is therefore not considered an error in the current year. Thus, utilization of the iron curtain approach can result in a misstatement in the current year income statement not being evaluated as an error at all.

Companies must quantify the impact of correcting all misstatements, including both the carryover and reversing effects of prior year misstatements, on the current year financial statements. This can be accomplished by quantifying an error under both the rollover and iron curtain approaches and by evaluating the error measured under each approach. Thus, a company's financial statements would require adjustment when either approach results in quantifying a misstatement that is material, after considering all relevant quantitative and qualitative factors.

It is possible that correcting an error in the current year could materially misstate the current year's income statement. For example, correcting the $100 misstatement in the current year will:

- Correct the $20 error originating in the current year;
- Correct the $80 balance sheet carryover error that originated in Years 1 through 4; but also
- Misstate the current year income statement by $80.

If the $80 understatement of current year expense is material to the current year, after all of the relevant quantitative and qualitative factors are considered, the prior year financial statements should be corrected, even though such revision previously was and continues to be immaterial to the prior year financial statements.

Accounting Changes and Error Corrections Disclosures

There are a number of variations on the disclosures required for the various types of accounting changes and error corrections, so we address each one within the following sub-sections.

Change in Accounting Principle

When there is a change in accounting principle, disclose all of the following items in the period in which the change takes place:

- *Nature of the change.* The nature of the change and why the new principle is preferable.
- *Application method.* State the method used to apply the change, including:
    - The information being adjusted
    - The effect of the change on income from continuing operations, net income, any other affected financial statement line items, and any affected per-share amounts
    - The cumulative effect of the change on retained earnings in the balance sheet as of the beginning of the earliest period presented
    - The reasons why retrospective application is impracticable (if this is the case), and the alternative method used to report the change

- *Indirect effects.* If the election has been made to recognize the indirect effects of a change in principle, disclose the effects, the amounts recognized in the current period, any applicable per-share amounts, and the same information for all prior periods presented (unless impracticable to do so).

These disclosures are required for all interim and annual financial statements that are reported.

When a new accounting principle is adopted, disclose the effect of the change on income from continuing operations, net income, and any related per-share amounts for all remaining interim periods in the current fiscal year.

SAMPLE DISCLOSURE

In 20X1, we adopted amended standards that simplify how entities test goodwill for impairment. These amended standards permit an assessment of qualitative factors to determine whether it is more likely than not that the fair value of a reporting unit in which goodwill resides is less than its carrying value. For reporting units in which this assessment concludes that it is more likely than not that the fair value is more than its carrying value, these amended standards eliminate the requirement to perform goodwill impairment testing. The adoption of these amended standards did not have an impact on our consolidated financial statements.

Change in Accounting Estimate

If there is a change in estimate that will affect several future periods, disclose the effect on income from continuing operations, net income, and any related per-share amounts. This disclosure is not needed for ongoing changes in estimate that arise in the ordinary course of business, such as changes in reserves. In effect, this disclosure is only required if the change is material. If there is not an immediate material effect, but a material effect is expected in later periods, provide a description of the change in estimate.

SAMPLE DISCLOSURE

The Company uses valuation techniques in order to determine the fair value of derivative financial instruments. During 20X2 we revisited the approach of including the basis spread in our calculation of the fair value of derivative instruments to better reflect the contract terms under the current market conditions. As a result of this change in estimate, a gain of $800,000 was recognized in net income.

SAMPLE DISCLOSURE

In 20X2, the Company evaluated the useful life criteria for its oil tankers and concluded that the average useful life assumption should be reduced by 2.5 years. This change in estimate resulted in an accelerated rate of depreciation, which resulted in a charge of $1,700,000 against net income.

Change in Reporting Entity

In those rare cases where there has been a change in reporting entity, disclose the nature of and reason for the change. In addition, report the effect of the change on income, net income, other comprehensive income, and any related per-share amounts for all periods presented. If there is not an immediate material effect, but a material effect is expected in later periods, state the nature of and reason for the change in the period in which the change occurred.

SAMPLE DISCLOSURE

In August 20X3, Coronary Associates resigned as the sole corporate member of the Ekaterina-Klingman General Hospital (EKG), and no longer controls the activities and affairs of EKG. The replacement of EKG has been accounted for as a change in reporting entity; therefore, the 20X1 and 20X2 combined financial statements have been adjusted to exclude the financial position and activities of EKG.

Error Corrections

When the financial statements are restated to correct an error, disclose the following information:

- A statement that the previously issued financial statements have been restated, and describe the error
- The effect of the error correction on financial statement line items and per-share amounts for each period presented
- The cumulative effect of the error correction on retained earnings as of the beginning of the earliest period presented

- The before-tax and after-tax effect on net income for each prior period reported. If the results of only one period are reported, indicate the effect on net income for the immediately preceding period

If there is an error correction related to prior interim periods of the current fiscal year, disclose the effect on income from continuing operations, net income, and related per-share amounts for all of the prior interim periods of the current fiscal year, as well as the restated results for these line items.

SAMPLE DISCLOSURE

Subsequent to the original issuance of the Company's annual consolidated financial statements, the Company determined that certain revenue transactions were previously recognized in the Company's consolidated financial statements prior to meeting relevant revenue recognition criteria. These transactions relate to bill and hold transactions for which there was not sufficient supporting documentation to establish that revenue had been earned. The restatement of the Company's consolidated financial statements reflects a correction of revenue to include only those bill and hold transactions with complete supporting documentation.

SAMPLE DISCLOSURE

During the fiscal year ended December 31, 20X3, the Company discovered that it had improperly recognized fixed assets during the fiscal year ended December 31, 20X1. The correction of this error reduced beginning net assets by $247,000 and required a restatement of fiscal year 20X2 financial statements as reflected in the income statement, balance sheet, and statement of cash flows.

Prior Period Adjustments

If there is a material retroactive prior period adjustment made during any interim period, disclosure must be made of the effect on net income and earnings per share of any prior period included in the report, as well as on retained earnings.

Historical Summaries

If a business issues historical summaries of its results for a number of prior years, be sure to adjust these summaries for any errors found in the affected years, and disclose the changes alongside the summaries.

EXAMPLE

Armadillo Industries provides the following disclosure regarding a change in its method of accounting for the valuation of its inventory:

> On January 1, 20X1, Armadillo changed its method for valuing inventory to the weighted-average method. The company had previously used the LIFO method to value its inventory. The new method was adopted because management felt that having very old inventory layers misrepresented the value of the company's reported inventory. The company's comparative financial statements for previous years have been adjusted to apply the new method retrospectively.

> The following financial statement line items for fiscal years 20X1 and 20X0 were affected by this change in accounting principle:

20X1 Income Statement

	As Computed under LIFO	As Reported under Weighted Average	Effect of Change
Sales	$1,000,000	$1,000,000	$0
Cost of goods sold	600,000	580,000	20,000
Selling, general and administrative expenses	375,000	375,000	0
Income before taxes	25,000	45,000	20,000
Income taxes	9,000	16,000	-7,000
Net income	$16,000	$29,000	$13,000

20X0 Income Statement

	As Originally Reported	As Adjusted	Effect of Change
Sales	$900,000	$900,000	$0
Cost of goods sold	540,000	525,000	15,000
Selling, general and administrative expenses	350,000	350,000	0
Income before taxes	10,000	25,000	15,000
Income taxes	3,000	9,000	-6,000
Net income	$7,000	$16,000	$9,000

16

20X1 Balance Sheet

	As Computed under LIFO	As Reported under Weighted Average	Effect of Change
Cash	$100,000	$100,000	$0
Accounts receivable	350,000	350,000	0
Inventory	400,000	420,000	20,000
Total assets	$850,000	$870,000	$20,000
Accounts payable	$125,000	$125,000	$0
Income tax liability	9,000	16,000	7,000
Paid-in capital	500,000	500,000	0
Retained earnings	216,000	229,000	13,000
Total liabilities and stockholders' equity	$850,000	$870,000	$20,000

20X0 Balance Sheet

	As Originally Reported	As Adjusted	Effect of Change
Cash	$80,000	$80,000	$0
Accounts receivable	320,000	320,000	0
Inventory	360,000	375,000	15,000
Total assets	$760,000	$775,000	$15,000
Accounts payable	$100,000	$100,000	$0
Income tax liability	3,000	9,000	6,000
Paid-in capital	500,000	500,000	0
Retained earnings	157,000	166,000	9,000
Total liabilities and stockholders' equity	$760,000	$775,000	$15,000

Summary

Retrospective changes can require detailed detective work, judgment, and thorough documentation of the changes made. Given the amount of labor involved, it is cost-effective to find justifiable reasons for not making retrospective changes. Two valid methods for doing so are to question the materiality of the necessary changes, or to find reasons to instead treat issues as changes in accounting estimate.

If retrospective application is completely unavoidable, it may make sense to have the company's auditors review proposed retrospective changes in advance. Doing so minimizes the risk that an issue will be discovered by the auditors during the annual audit, which will require additional retrospective changes. When working with the auditors in advance in this manner, fully document the discussion; otherwise, either or both parties may have forgotten essential elements of the retrospective application by the time the annual audit occurs, which could be many months later.

Glossary

A

Accounting change. A change in accounting principle, estimate, or reporting entity.

Accounting principles. The rules and guidelines that an entity must follow when reporting financial information.

C

Change in accounting estimate. An alteration that adjusts or will adjust the carrying amount of assets or liabilities. It is derived from new information.

Change in accounting principle. A switch from the use of one generally accepted accounting principle to another, when there is a choice of principle.

F

Fiscal year. The 12-month period over which an entity reports on the activities that appear in its annual financial statements.

I

Interim period. A financial reporting period that is shorter than a full fiscal year.

P

Prospective application. When a change is applied on a go-forward basis. No adjustments are made to prior periods.

R

Restatement. The revision of previous financial statements when they are found to contain a material error.

Retrospective application. When a principle must be used as the basis for creating financial statements as though the principle had always been used for all periods presented.

Index

www.ingramcontent.com/pod-product-compliance
Lightning Source LLC
Chambersburg PA
CBHW051432200326
41520CB00023B/7439